THE SWIMMING PARENT'S GUIDE TO IMPROVED NUTRITION BY ENHANCING YOUR RMR:

Finding Newer and Better Ways to Feed Your Body and Increase Muscle Growth Naturally

By

Joseph Correa

Certified Sports Nutritionist

COPYRIGHT

ACKNOWLEDGEMENTS

The realization and success of this book could not have been possible without the motivation and support of my family.

THE SWIMMING PARENT'S GUIDE TO IMPROVED NUTRITION BY ENHANCING YOUR RMR:

Finding Newer and Better Ways to Feed Your Body and Increase Muscle Growth Naturally

By

Joseph Correa

Certified Sports Nutritionist

CONTENTS

Copyright

Acknowledgements

About The Author

WHAT WILL THIS NUTRITION GUIDE DO FOR ME?

INTRODUCTION

CHAPTER 1: The Swimming Parent's Guide to Improved Nutrition by Enhancing Your RMR

Finding newer and better ways to feed your body and increase muscle growth naturally

CHAPTER 2: Eat, Sleep, Breathe Your Way to a Leaner Body

Your secret weapon RMR

CHAPTER 3: How to Get in Shape 24 Hours a Day

Accelerating your metabolism to enhance performance

CHAPTER 4: Better Swimming Performance through Antioxidants

Change your nutritional lifestyle now to get long term results and faster recovery times

CHAPTER 5: You Are What You Eat

Commit to improving your mind and body

CHAPTER 6: Increase Your Protein with Homemade Protein Meals for Swimming

Taking the next step to see results

ABOUT THE AUTHOR

As a certified sports nutritionist and professional athlete, I traveled around the world and competed against some of the best. Being able to share what I have learned is important to me. My knowledge and experience has helped my students throughout the years. The more you know about what to feed your body, the better you will do.

If you want to see long term results in a healthy and realistic manner, than this book will do that for you.

Adding supplements or performance enhancers is a decision you have to make on your own. Always consider what side effects or long term changes your body will have before starting since that should be your primary concern. Finding organic and natural sources are always a better alternative.

WHAT WILL THIS NUTRITION GUIDE DO FOR ME?

This book is the key to helping you achieve your goals. Joseph Correa, a certified sports nutritionist and a professional athlete who has dedicated himself to improving his performance through better nutrition and quality training exercises. Through his extensive knowledge and experience has created this easy to understand book on improved nutrition. He is convinced of the importance of proper nutrition and exercise to see long term results.

This book was created as a step by step and easy to follow guide to getting in shape. To get the most out of it follow these simple steps:

Try not to skip any chapters as they go in order so that you can use the knowledge from one chapter to better understand the content in other chapters.

INTRODUCTION

The Swimming Parent's Guide to Improved Nutrition by Enhancing Your RMR will show you how to increase your RMR (resting metabolic rate) to accelerate your metabolism and help you change your body for good. Your Resting Metabolic Rate measures the amount of energy used by your body in a resting or relaxed state. RMR is your greatest component of energy expenditure in your body and so it tells us just how much energy and fat your body burns on a daily basis. By adding lean muscle mass you automatically increase your RMR which can lead to improved performance with long lasting results.

This book will teach you how to add lean muscle mass in order to increase your RMR and accelerate your metabolism. Eating complex carbohydrates, protein, and natural fats in the right amount and percentages as well as increasing your RMR will make you faster, stronger, and more resistant.

If you want to make a serious change on your body and how it performs on a daily basis, you need to read this book and start applying it in your daily life.

Not knowing where to start or when to start is not an excuse. Take your nutrition seriously and see just where it takes you.

When you increase your RMR you will find you:

- Have more energy before, during, and after training or competing.
- Add more lean muscle mass.
- Reduce injuries and muscle cramps.
- Have more focus and are better able to stay concentrated for longer periods of time.
- Reduce fat at an accerated rate.

Joseph Correa is a certified sports nutritionist and a professional athlete.

CHAPTER 1

THE SWIMMING PARENT'S GUIDE TO IMPROVED NUTRITION BY ENHANCING YOUR RMR

Finding newer and better ways to feed your body and increase muscle growth naturally

This nutrition plan will help you reach this and many of your nutrition goals so that you can get the most out of your body. This nutrition guide serves as a perfect base for any athlete who wants to reach peak performance for the long term and be able to maintain it over the years. You will see long lasting results as an athlete primarily because of the focus on organic energy sources. This will allow you to perform at your very best for the longest period of time without any future negative effects on the brain and body unlike some enhanced performance substances that will strip the body of the essential elements to create natural processes in the body and alter them to create short term improvements.

All athletes should eat a lot of fruit, vegetables, and protein derived foods (chicken, eggs, turkey, fish, etc.). Complex carbohydrates intake should be cut down to a maximum of brown rice, pasta, all natural bread, and organic ingredients. In some places around the world where people have the longest life spans we can see several things in common: they drink mostly water, natural fruit juices, and milk. Everything they eat and drink is composed of natural, non-processed, non-canned, and non-preservative containing foods. By using this knowledge about people with longer life spans and their eating habits and other medical facts, I have created a nutrition guide that will help you to live and compete healthier and to live longer. It will also allow you to control your weight and the shape of your body better.

This is not your typical diet book where you're told about a magical drink that makes you lose weight or pills that make you lose 10 pounds in a week. There are also diets that focus on not eating almost anything at all. Many of these diets have a negative long term effect on your mind and body. <u>The truth is there is NO magic formula!</u> The key to getting in better shape is simply eating right and exercising. Doing those two things the right way is what this book is about.

Why are we focusing on the answer to your problems first?

Knowing what needs to be done does not guarantee that you'll know what steps need to be taken to get there!

Why do we have such a serious obesity and malnutrition problem around the world and why has it become with the youngsters as well?

There's always something in life that you end up neglecting and later regretting. This is specifically true with health. Usually, physical problems start small and then go on to become very difficult to manage and that's why we need to prevent them starting with our youth.

Getting Some Perspective

I try to think of life in very basic terms. If you leave out all of the technological advances that clutter our lives and focus on a more basic lifestyle you will find yourself in a very different environment. What do I mean by this? *Well, let's say we didn't have TV, internet, or cell phones. Let's say there are no cars, planes or escalators. No more hot dogs, hamburgers, soft drinks, and junk food (these are not technological advances but we'll throw them in as well)*. Please don't faint! I know most of us can't live without many of these things but we are just trying to put things into perspective. What have you got left in terms of food? We will still have fruits and vegetables that come from plants and trees. We still have meat in the form of chicken, beef, fish, and pork. But guess what? We may have to hunt for fish or other animals we want to eat and that involves doing physical exercise. We have to walk, climb, and stretch to pick mangoes or apples off trees. All this requires that we walk, run, or otherwise burn more calories.

Now, once we catch or harvest our food we have to prepare it. Do we have a microwave or oven to cook the food? No, but we may have a pan or pot to heat with fire. You might also catch some sun while hunting and picking fruits. Do you know how important a little sun can be to your health? Let's use an example.

In tropical waters, in some parts of the world, pink dolphins exist. As strange as this may sound there is a very logical explanation. These dolphins live in areas of high density of tropical plant life where very little sunlight comes through into the water. Because of this deficiency in sunlight, their skin has become almost transparent and that gives dolphins a pinkish appearance. You have to see it to believe it, but the point is that you need a little sun as well, so try to get some sun every once in a while. Don't overdo it! Just enough sun is good enough.

I know this is an unusual way of thinking but at least now we know how simple we can make our daily lives while becoming healthier. I am not saying you should live like this, but, you should try to apply some of these basic ideas that have been forgotten due to changes in our society and technological advances. You might decide to walk to the grocery store to buy food and get a workout while doing so. You might decide to park a little further away at work so that you have to do some extra walking. When you're at the park with your kids, jog with them or go swimming over the weekend as a family. Instead of preparing food or eating food prepared with a lot of oil or butter, try boiling it, using the oven, or steam cooking.

Do your best to make sure that the majority of what you eat has a strong nutritional value and is as fresh as possible. This will help you stay healthy and fit, for years to come.

This book is divided into 3 swimming lifestyles:

Low Cardio Lifestyle Athlete (LCLA):

This dietary phase is for athletes who require less food containing complex carbohydrates (these include but are not limited to: pasta, brown rice, oatmeal, brown beans, lentils, etc.). These people do not need to store up that many energy reserves and therefore should have a higher percentage of foods containing proteins, legumes, vegetables, dairies fruits and other.

LCLA is for athletes who don't do more than 30 minutes of cardio per day as part of their training and also during competition. You can be flexible during competition since some conditions and environmental changes might change just how you can absorb food. This could be because of the country you are competing in, or you might feel nauseous before competing, or it can also be because of the food available in that area.

After the first month of completing this diet phase and complementing it in combination with your regular physical training regiment, you can decide to continue or adapt the diet to your needs in case you feel you need to add more protein or carbs or dairies.

Medium Cardio Lifestyle Athlete (MCLA):

This dietary phase is for athletes who require a specific percentage of foods containing complex carbohydrates (these include but are not limited to: pasta, brown rice, oatmeal, brown beans, lentils, etc.) to maintain a medium cardio-intensive lifestyle, while at the same time consuming a higher percentage of foods containing proteins, dairies, legumes, and fruits.

MCLA is for athletes who complete a minimum of 30 minutes of cardiovascular workouts as part of their daily physical training which may include (if you cross-train): swimming, walking, running, bicycling, jumping, rowing or playing sports that combine any of the aforementioned activities.

High Cardio Lifestyle Athlete (HCLA):

This dietary phase is for athletes who require a larger percentage of foods containing complex carbs to maintain their cardio intensive lifestyles in a balanced and healthy manner, while still maintaining a high percentage of foods containing protein, legumes, vegetables, fruits, and nuts.

HCLA is for people who train more than an hour of daily cardiovascular exercise. At least one hour of high intensity cardio workouts include (if you cross-train): running, swimming, rowing, jumping, or bicycling. This is especially important for athletes who do a lot of cardiovascular exercise as they require more carbohydrates to stay in good physical shape and to allow their bodies to recover.

The USDA Food guide pyramid contains the following groups of food.

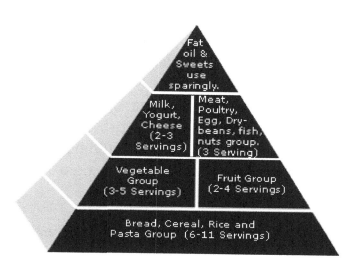

a) Bread, Cereals, Rice, Pasta Group (6 to 11 servings): This group consists of the carbohydrate heavy foods and is placed at the bottom of the pyramid indicating that they should be eaten more often and should form an important part of the daily diet. The rationale behind eating more carbohydrates is that they provide energy so that a person is required to eat less fat. It is recommended that a person should have 6-11 servings from this group.

b) Vegetables (3-5 servings) and Fruit (2-4 servings): There is no doubt that fruit and vegetables are good for the body. Fruit and vegetables provide the body with essential vitamins and other nutrients and ward off diseases and ailments. A person should have 3-5 servings of vegetables and 2-4 servings of fruit a day.

c) Meat, Poultry, Fish, Dry Beans, Eggs and Nuts Group (2-3 servings): This group provides the body with proteins. Proteins help in building the body tissues and muscles. A person should eat 2-3 servings from this group a day.

d) Milk, Yogurt and Cheese Group (2-3 servings): This group provides proteins and calcium that make the bones strong and prevent health problems related to the degeneration of bone mass. A person should eat 2-3 servings from this group a day.

e) Fats, Oils and Sweets (eat sparingly): This group should be eaten sparingly. Fat leads to heart disease and obesity. Too much sugar also leads to obesity which can later create health problems in the future.

The food guide pyramid provides an excellent way to ensure that the body's nutritional requirements are fulfilled properly. By following the guide, an individual will receive all the daily requirements in terms of energy, proteins, vitamins and other essential nutrients.

Here are the recommended sizes of the servings for foods high in carbohydrates.

Vegetables: 1 cup of raw vegetables, or ½ a cup of cooked vegetables, or ¾s of a cup of vegetable juice.

Fruit: 1 medium sized fruit (such as 1 medium sized apple or 1 medium sized orange), ½ a cup of a canned or chopped fruit, or ¾s of a cup of fruit juice.

Bread and cereals: 1 slice of bread; 1 ounce or 2/3 s of a cup of ready-to-eat cereal; ½ a cup of cooked rice, pasta, or cereal; ½ a cup of cooked dry beans, lentils, or dried peas.

Dairy: 1 cup of skimmed or low fat milk.

The proper intake of proteins, fats and carbohydrates for non-athletes is:

Proteins 12%

Carbohydrates 58%

Fats 30%

The proper intake of proteins, fats and carbohydrates for athletes is:

Proteins 15-25%

Carbohydrates 50-65%

Fats 10-25%

Body builders eat more proteins to add muscle and bulk, with the proteins accounting for up to 35-40% of the diet for professional body builders.

Aerobic vs Anaerobic Physical Activity:

There are 2 main types of physical activity: Aerobic activity and anaerobic activity.

Anaerobic activity is defined as the activity undertaken without the presence of oxygen which cannot be sustained for long periods of time. This type of activity relies heavily on the fast twitch muscle fibers. Examples of anaerobic activity are weight lifting and sprinting. Such activities cannot be undertaken for long periods of time. This type of activity helps in building lean tissue and improves the body composition. The anaerobic capacity test is a test that measures the ability of the body to undertake exercise of a short duration and of a very high intensity. The Wingate cycle test is commonly used to test anaerobic capacity. Aerobic Fitness, also known as cardiovascular fitness is the ability of the body to perform an exercise over an extended period of time in the presence of oxygen. This type of activity relies heavily on slow twitch muscle fibers.

A training program which combines cardiovascular fitness and muscular fitness allows more oxygenated blood to be delivered per beat and increases the myoglobin in the muscles so that they can take up more amounts of oxygen, thus allowing more work to be done. This is why it is a smart decision to cross train. In swimming, being able to combine both aerobic with anaerobic training will give you the best results before, during, and after competition.

SOME OF THE FOODS THAT ARE TO BE USED FOR NUTRITION PLAN ARE:

Complex Carbohydrates

(Each portion is considered 1 serving)

Morning Carbs (1 cup)

Oatmeal

2 slices of toast

Raisin bran cereal

Oat bran cereal

Whole-wheat cereal

Half a wheat bagel

Half a slice pita bread

1 bran muffin

1 wheat waffle

1 wheat pancake

Mid-day Carbs (1/2 cup)

Brown rice

Pasta

1 slice of wheat toast

Wheat pasta

Wild rice

1 sweet potato

1 baked potato

Black, Kidney and Red beans

Lentils

Peas

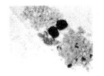

Proteins

(Each portion is considered 1 serving)

No more than 3 dark meats per week and a minimum of

3 types of fish per week.

Morning Proteins	Mid-day proteins	Afternoon Proteins
4 egg whites	4 egg whites	Salmon 4 oz.
Ham 4 oz.	Ham 4 oz.	Ham 4 oz.
Fish (any) 4 oz.	Fish (any) 4 oz.	Fish (any) 4 oz.
1 can of tuna	1 can of tuna	1 can of tuna
Slices of turkey 4oz.	Turkey 4 oz.	Turkey 4 oz
1 cup of shrimp	1 cup of shrimp	Tilapia 4 oz.
Steak or red meat 4 oz.	Steak or red meat 4 oz.	Steak or red meat 2 oz.
1 strip of bacon	Pork 4 oz.	Pork 2 oz.
Chicken or other poultry 4 oz.	Chicken or other poultry 4 oz	Chicken or other poultry 4 oz.

Seafood *(Nutritional Facts)*

Cooked (by moist or dry heat with no added ingredients), edible weight portion.
Percent Daily Values (%DV) are based on a 2,000 calorie diet.

Seafood Serving Size (84 g/3 oz)	Calories	Calories from Fat	Total Fat (g)	(%DV)	Saturated Fat (g)	(%DV)	Cholesterol (mg)	(%DV)	Sodium (mg)	(%DV)	Potassium (mg)	(%DV)	Total Carbohydrate (g)	(%DV)	Protein (g)	(%DV)	Vitamin A (%DV)	Vitamin C (%DV)	Calcium (%DV)	Iron (%DV)
Blue Crab	100	10	1	2	0	0	95	32	330	14	300	9	0	0	20	0	4		10	4
Catfish	130	60	6	9	2	10	50	17	40	2	230	7	0	0	17	0	0	0	0	0
Clams, about 12 small	110	15	1.5	2	0	0	80	27	95	4	470	13	6	2	17	10	0	8	30	
Cod	90	5	1	2	0	0	50	17	65	3	460	13	0	0	20	0	2	2	2	
Flounder/Sole	100	15	1.5	2	0	0	55	18	100	4	390	11	0	0	19	0	0	2	0	
Haddock	100	10	1	2	0	0	70	23	85	4	340	10	0	0	21	2	0	2	6	
Halibut	120	15	2	3	0	0	40	13	60	3	500	14	0	0	23	4	0	2	6	
Lobster	80	0	0.5	1	0	0	60	20	320	13	300	9	1	0	17	2	0	6	2	
Ocean Perch	110	20	2	3	0.5	3	45	15	95	4	290	8	0	0	21	0	2	10	4	
Orange Roughy	80	5	1	2	0	0	20	7	70	3	340	10	0	0	16	2	0	4	2	
Oysters, about 12 medium	100	35	4	6	1	5	80	27	300	13	220	6	6	2	10	0	6	6	45	
Pollock	90	10	1	2	0	0	80	27	110	5	370	11	0	0	20	2	0	0	2	
Rainbow Trout	140	50	6	9	2	10	55	18	35	1	370	11	0	0	20	4	4	8	2	
Rockfish	110	15	2	3	0	0	40	13	70	3	440	13	0	0	21	4	0	2	2	
Salmon, Atlantic/Coho /Sockeye /Chinook	200	90	10	15	2	10	70	23	55	2	430	12	0	0	24	4	4	2	2	
Salmon, Chum/Pink	130	40	4	6	1	5	70	23	65	3	420	12	0	0	22	2	0	2	4	
Scallops, about 6 large or 14 small	140	10	1	2	0	0	65	22	310	13	430	12	5	2	27	2	0	4	14	
Shrimp	100	10	1.5	2	0	0	170	57	240	10	220	6	0	0	21	4	4	6	10	

Swordfish	120	50	6	9	1.5	8	40	13	100	4	310	9	0	0	16	2	2	0	6
Tilapia	110	20	2.5	4	1	5	75	25	30	1	360	10	0	0	22	0	2	0	2
Tuna	130	15	1.5	2	0	0	50	17	40	2	480	14	0	0	26	2	2	2	4

Source: U.S. Food and Drug Administration

Vegetables and Legumes

(1-2 cups total of any below)

Vary between raw leafy vegetables, cooked vegetables, and vegetable juice

Morning V & L's	Mid-day V & L's	Afternoon V & L's
Lettuce	Lettuce	Lettuce
Tomato	Tomato	Tomato
Carrots	Broccoli	Broccoli
Spinach	Carrots	Carrots
Green Peas	Spinach	Spinach
Corn	Green peas	Green peas
Celery	Corn	Corn
Cucumber	Celery	Celery
Vegetable juice	Cucumber	Cucumber
Squash	Vegetable juice	Vegetable juice
String beans	Squash	Squash
Mushrooms	String beans	String beans
Sprouts	Cauliflower	Cauliflower
Beets	Mushrooms	Mushrooms
	Cabbage	Cabbage
	Peppers	Peppers
	Sprouts	Sprouts
	Beets	Beets

Vegetables *(Nutritional Facts)*

Raw, edible weight portion. Percent Daily Values (%DV) are based on a 2,000 calorie diet.

Vegetables Serving Size (gram weight/ ounce weight)	Calories	Calories from Fat	Total Fat (g)	(%DV)	Sodium (mg)	(%DV)	Potassium (mg)	(%DV)	Total Carbohydrates (g)	(%DV)	Dietary Fiber (g)	(%DV)	Sugars (g)	Protein (g)	Vitamin A (%DV)	Vitamin C (%DV)	Calcium (%DV)	Iron (%DV)
Asparagus 5 spears (93 g/3.3 oz)	20	0	0	0	0	0	230	7	4	1	2	8	2	2	10	15	2	2
Bell Pepper 1 medium (148 g/5.3 oz)	25	0	0	0	40	2	220	6	6	2	2	8	4	1	4	190	2	4
Broccoli 1 medium stalk (148 g/5.3 oz)	45	0	0.5	1	80	3	460	13	8	3	3	12	2	4	6	220	6	6
Carrot 1 carrot, 7" long, 1 1/4" diameter (78 g/2.8 oz)	30	0	0	0	60	3	250	7	7	2	2	8	5	1	110	10	2	2
Cauliflower 1/6 medium head (99 g/3.5 oz)	25	0	0	0	30	1	270	8	5	2	2	8	2	2	0	100	2	2
Celery 2 medium stalks (110 g/3.9 oz)	15	0	0	0	115	5	260	7	4	1	2	8	2	0	10	15	4	2
Cucumber 1/3 medium (99 g/3.5 oz)	10	0	0	0	0	0	140	4	2	1	1	4	1	1	4	10	2	2
Green (Snap) Beans 3/4 cup cut (83 g/3.0 oz)	20	0	0	0	0	0	200	6	5	2	3	12	2	1	4	10	4	2
Green Cabbage 1/12 medium head (84 g/3.0 oz)	25	0	0	0	20	1	190	5	5	2	2	8	3	1	0	70	4	2
Green Onion 1/4 cup chopped (25 g/0.9 oz)	10	0	0	0	10	0	70	2	2	1	1	4	1	0	2	8	2	2

Vegetable																		
Iceberg Lettuce 1/6 medium head (89 g/3.2 oz)	10	0	0	0	10	0	125	4	2	1	1	4	2	1	6	6	2	2
Leaf Lettuce 1 1/2 cups shredded (85 g/3.0 oz)	15	0	0	0	35	1	170	5	2	1	1	4	1	1	130	6	2	4
Mushrooms 5 medium (84 g/3.0 oz)	20	0	0	0	15	0	300	9	3	1	1	4	0	3	0	2	0	2
Onion 1 medium (148 g/5.3 oz)	45	0	0	0	5	0	190	5	11	4	3	12	9	1	0	20	4	4
Potato 1 medium (148 g/5.3 oz)	110	0	0	0	0	0	620	18	26	9	2	8	1	3	0	45	2	6
Radishes 7 radishes (85 g/3.0 oz)	10	0	0	0	55	2	190	5	3	1	1	4	2	0	0	30	2	2
Summer Squash 1/2 medium (98 g/3.5 oz)	20	0	0	0	0	0	260	7	4	1	2	8	2	1	6	30	2	2
Sweet Corn kernels from 1 medium ear (90 g/3.2 oz)	90	20	2.5	4	0	0	250	7	18	6	2	8	5	4	2	10	0	2
Sweet Potato 1 medium, 5" long, 2" diameter (130 g/4.6 oz)	100	0	0	0	70	3	440	13	23	8	4	16	7	2	120	30	4	4
Tomato 1 medium (148 g/5.3 oz)	25	0	0	0	20	1	340	10	5	2	1	4	3	1	20	40	2	4

Source: U.S. Food and Drug Administration

Fruits, Nuts, and Seeds *(Vary between raw fruit, frozen fruit, fruit juice, and dried fruit.)*

Fruits (1-2 cups)	Nuts (1-2 table spoons)	Seeds other (1-2 table spoons)
Apples	Peanuts	Sunflower seeds
Pears	Cashews	Dried pumpkin seeds
Bananas	Walnuts	Flax seeds
Pineapple	Pistachio nuts	Sesame Seeds
Oranges	Almonds	Avocado
Tangerines	Hazel nuts	Black olives
Grapefruit	Brazilian nuts	Green olives
Blackberries	Pecans	Flaxseed oil
Blueberries	Macadamia nuts	Canola oil
Strawberries		Olive oil
Plums		
Peaches		
Cherries		
Passion fruit		
Papaya		
Kiwi		
Cantaloupe		
Watermelon		
Fruit juice		

Fruits *(Nutritional Facts)*

Raw, edible weight portion. Percent Daily Values (%DV) are based on a 2,000 calorie diet.

Fruits Serving Size (gram weight/ounce weight)	Calories	Calories from Fat	Total Fat (g)	(%DV)	Sodium (mg)	(%DV)	Potassium (mg)	(%DV)	Total Carbohydrate (g)	(%DV)	Dietary Fiber (g)	(%DV)	Sugars (g)	Protein (g)	Vitamin A (%DV)	Vitamin C (%DV)	Calcium (%DV)	Iron (%DV)
Apple 1 large (242 g/8 oz)	130	0	0	0	0	0	260	7	34	11	5	20	25	1	2	8	2	2
Avocado California, 1/5 medium (30 g/1.1 oz)	50	35	4.5	7	0	0	140	4	3	1	1	4	0	1	0	4	0	2
Banana 1 medium (126 g/4.5 oz)	110	0	0	0	0	0	450	13	30	10	3	12	19	1	2	15	0	2
Cantaloupe 1/4 medium (134 g/4.8 oz)	50	0	0	0	20	1	240	7	12	4	1	4	11	1	120	80	2	2
Grapefruit 1/2 medium (154 g/5.5 oz)	60	0	0	0	0	0	160	5	15	5	2	8	11	1	35	100	4	0
Grapes 3/4 cup (126 g/4.5 oz)	90	0	0	0	15	1	240	7	23	8	1	4	20	0	0	2	2	0
Honeydew-Melon 1/10 medium melon (134 g/4.8 oz)	50	0	0	0	30	1	210	6	12	4	1	4	11	1	2	45	2	2
Kiwifruit 2 medium (148 g/5.3 oz)	90	10	1	2	0	0	450	13	20	7	4	16	13	1	2	240	4	2
Lemon 1 medium (58 g/2.1 oz)	15	0	0	0	0	0	75	2	5	2	2	8	2	0	0	40	2	0
Lime 1 medium (67 g/2.4 oz)	20	0	0	0	0	0	75	2	7	2	2	8	0	0	0	35	0	0

Food																	
Nectarine 1 medium (140 g/5.0 oz)	60	5	0.5	1	0	0	250	7	15	5	2	8	11	1	8	15	0	2
Orange 1 medium (154 g/5.5 oz)	80	0	0	0	0	0	250	7	19	6	3	12	14	1	2	130	6	0
Peach 1 medium (147 g/5.3 oz)	60	0	0.5	1	0	0	230	7	15	5	2	8	13	1	6	15	0	2
Pear 1 medium (166 g/5.9 oz)	100	0	0	0	0	0	190	5	26	9	6	24	16	1	0	10	2	0
Pineapple 2 slices, 3" diameter, 3/4" thick (112 g/4 oz)	50	0	0	0	10	0	120	3	13	4	1	4	10	1	2	50	2	2
Plums 2 medium (151 g/5.4 oz)	70	0	0	0	0	0	230	7	19	6	2	8	16	1	8	10	0	2
Strawberries 8 medium (147 g/5.3 oz)	50	0	0	0	0	0	170	5	11	4	2	8	8	1	0	160	2	2
Sweet Cherries 21 cherries; 1 cup (140 g/5.0 oz)	100	0	0	0	0	0	350	10	26	9	1	4	16	1	2	15	2	2
Tangerine 1 medium (109 g/3.9 oz)	50	0	0	0	0	0	160	5	13	4	2	8	9	1	6	45	4	0
Watermelon 1/18 medium melon; 2 cups diced pieces (280 g/10.0 oz)	80	0	0	0	0	0	270	8	21	7	1	4	20	1	30	25	2	4

Dairy Foods and Snacks (Each is 1 serving)
Preferably low-fat dairies

(Each is 1 serving)

Preferably low-fat dairies

Dairy Foods

1 cup of milk (8 oz.)

1 cup of soy milk (8 oz.)

Low fat cheese (2 slices)

½ cup cottage cheese

1 cup low fat yogurt (8 oz.)

¼ cup low fat mozzarella cheese

¼ cup soy cheese

1 low fat ice cream yogurt bar

1 cup low fat fruit yogurt (8 oz.)

Snacks

1 fruit bar

One fruit (1/2 c

Dark chocolate (1 table spoon)

1 multigrain bar

5 low salt crackers

1 protein bar

Pretzels (1/2 cup)

Popcorn (1 2 cup)

1 low-fat rice cake

HELPFUL TIPS:

➢ Keep any condiments in your food to a minimum of one teaspoon per meal. Just enough to give your food some flavor.

➢ Instead of sugar, use honey to sweeten your drinks and food. If you absolutely have to use sugar make sure it's brown sugar.

Sports nutrition is more than just what you eat;

It's when and how you eat!

Drink at least 6-8 glasses of water per day

Drink 1 glass of water when you wake up, 1 before every meal, and 1 before going to sleep.

Eat 6 small to medium size meals per day

You should be eating every three hours. Use a timer, a stop watch or your cell phone to keep track of time as this is just as important as what you eat. If you eat small to medium size meals every three hours, you allow your body to digest food in an efficient manner and in a way that does not overwork the digestive system. Some people eat three large meals a day and then have to wait several hours until they don't feel full again but this is exactly what not to do.

Chew then swallow!

Sounds simple enough, but with today's busy schedules people tend to skip chewing and go directly to swallowing. That won't allow your body to process food the way it should, so make sure you take the time to chew your food. Your teeth have a purpose and that purpose is to break down food before it gets to your stomach so that it may do what it was intended to do. Remember, not chewing your food means your stomach has to work harder and that equates to a longer wait time for digestion that may cause you discomfort or gas.

No carbs or fruit after sunset

There's no need to store up energy you're not going to use while you sleep. Try to stay away from large meals after sunset. Be sure to consume a healthy snack if need be to prevent yourself from overeating during those times or simply drink a glass of water.

Always find time to exercise or do some form of stretching when you wake up, as this is the ideal time of day to get in shape and stay injury free.

Nutritional Guide for L C L A's

Monday – Saturday (daily percentage to be consumed)

20% complex carbs – 20% proteins – 30% vegetables and legumes – 15% fruits and nuts – 15% dairy foods and snacks

Or the equivalent in daily servings

Carbs (1-2 servings) – proteins (3-4 servings) – vegetables and legumes (3-6 servings) – Fruits and nuts (1.5-3 servings) – dairy foods and snacks (1.5 servings)

Sunday

(Some athletes don't train on Sundays or once a week so one day per week the food servings will change. We are using Sunday as that day.)

15% carbs – 25% proteins – 20% vegetables and legumes – 20% fruits and nuts – 20% dairy foods and snacks

Or the equivalent in servings

Carbs (1.5-3 servings) – proteins (2.5-3 servings) – vegetables and legumes (2 Servings) – Fruits and nuts (2-3 servings) – dairy foods and Snacks (2 servings)

*The percentages shown are for the daily consumption of these food groups and the servings are for the maximum amount of times you are allowed to consume these food groups. Follow the food group charts provided at the beginning of the book as a guide to what you can eat except for the dairies which you are free to choose the type and amount due to the variety of preferences and medical conditions out there.

Nutritional Guide for M C L A's

Monday - Saturday

15% carbs – 30% proteins – 25% vegetables and legumes – 15% fruits and nuts – 15% dairy foods and snacks

Or the equivalent in daily servings

Carbs (1.5-3 servings) – proteins (3-6 servings) – vegetables and legumes (2.5-6 servings) – Fruits and nuts (1.5-3 servings) – dairy foods and snacks (1.5-3 servings)

Sunday

(Some athletes don't train on Sundays or once a week so one day per week the food servings will change. We are using Sunday as that day.)

25% carbs – 20 % proteins – 20% vegetables and legumes – 20% fruits and nuts – 15% dairy foods and snacks

Or the equivalent in servings

Carbs (2.5-3 servings) – proteins (2-5 servings) – vegetables and legumes (2 servings) – Fruits and nuts (2 servings) – dairy foods and snacks (1.5 servings)

The percentages shown are for the daily consumption of these food groups and the servings are for the maximum amount of times you are allowed to consume these food groups. Follow the food group charts provided at the beginning of the book as a guide to what you can eat except for the dairies which you are free to choose the type and amount due to the variety of preferences and medical conditions out there.

Nutritional Guide for H C L A's

Monday - Saturday

20% carbs – 25% proteins – 20% vegetables and legumes – 15% fruits and nuts – 20% dairy foods and snacks

Or the equivalent in daily servings

Carbs (2 servings) – proteins (2.5 servings) – vegetables and legumes (2 servings) – Fruits and nuts (1.5 servings) – dairy foods and snacks (2 servings)

Sunday

(Some athletes don't train on Sundays or once a week so one day per week the food servings will change. We are using Sunday as that day.)

25% carbs – 20% proteins – 15% vegetables and legumes – 20% fruits and nuts – 20% dairy foods and snacks

Or the equivalent in servings

Carbs (2.5 servings) – proteins (2 servings) – vegetables and legumes (1.5 servings) – Fruits and nuts (2 servings) – dairy foods and snacks (2 servings)

*The percentages shown are for the daily consumption of these food groups and the servings are for the maximum amount of times you are allowed to consume these food groups. Follow the food group charts provided at the beginning of the book as a guide to what you can eat except for the dairies which you are free to choose the type and amount due to the variety of preferences and medical conditions out there.

CHAPTER 2

EAT, SLEEP, AND BREATHE YOUR WAY TO A LEANER BODY

Your Secret Weapon RMR

RMR is also known as resting metabolic rate and is the number of calories burned while your body is at rest because of normal body functions such as the heart rate and the breathing function. This accounts for 75% of the total calories burned during the day. This can vary from one person to another depending on age, amount of fat in your body, and other factors. The less fat you have in your body and the more muscle you have the higher the RMR will be and the faster you will burn calories at rest, even in your sleep. This is what some people consider as having a good metabolism but it really equates to having a high RMR. Having a high RMR will make you leaner and make easier for you to stay leaner every day. How to do you accomplish this? You can do this by changing what you eat to reduce fats and sugars, and by adding muscle to your body.

Each and every day is an opportunity to get back in shape. When you're tired of work and constantly busy with all the tedious things in life, you stop thinking about the importance of taking care of your body and mind. For this reason, I have prepared a daily schedule to help you <u>get in shape all day even while you eat, sleep, and breathe.</u> How is this possible? You can do this by simply by accelerating your metabolism. A natural way of doing this is by making small changes in your life that have an immediate effect on your body.

This daily schedule can be changed to accommodate your lifestyle as well as your training schedule. <u>Things you already do on a normal day will be highlighted in bold just to remind you that you're not really changing your day to day schedule at all.</u>

Remember, you are the only one that can keep yourself motivated enough to go through with the schedule. Working out every day and sticking to this nutrition guide requires sacrifice and being able to let go of temptations.

Temptations

Every day we pass by a pastry shop or a vending machine full of goodies. These are the moments you have to stay strong. Look away! Think of something else. Think of work. Think of your family. Think of how hard you're working to get and stay in shape. There's no one to stop you from eating a donut or a soft drink or potato chips, it's up to you to be disciplined. Every time you're able to withstand temptation, you'll be that much stronger. In case you've never done this before, don't go to the grocery store on an empty stomach as you will definitely buy things you should not be eating.

Stop smoking

Smoking WILL lower your life expectancy and more importantly it WILL decrease your quality of life! This nutrition guide should be used to improve your longevity and performance as an athlete through physical exercise and improved nutrition.

Smoking will work against you and your goals to improve your health habits.

Consume less alcohol

Drinking alcohol will dehydrate you much faster than most any other drinks so it would not be recommended you add this to your nutrition plan. Consult with your doctor to find out just how much is enough for you.

Improving your breathing techniques

Static breathing exercises, Yoga, Pilates, stretching, and other forms of breathing exercises will help you reduce your stress levels.

Less stress = A longer life

These exercises are for both men and women. They have changed my life and I am sure they will do the same for you. These are just some of the benefits you will see:

- Increased flexibility
- Stronger back and core muscles
- Improved posture
- Reduced stress

The Ideal Nutrition and Workout Schedule

Monday - Friday

7:00 AM   Drink one glass of water when you *wake up*.

7:15 AM   Complete a minimum of 5 abdominal exercises or 5 stretching exercises.

8:00 AM   Drink a glass of water, milk, or juice and then *eat breakfast*. Base your breakfast on the diet plan explained in chapter 1.

8:30 AM   Train as you normally would on a weekday.

10:00 AM   Drink one glass of water.

11:00 AM   Eat a fruit along with a multigrain bar (or another snack based on the list provided in chapter 1.). You can add or replace it with a yogurt or slices of a protein (turkey, ham, roast beef, fish, poultry, etc.).

11:10 AM   After having your snack make sure to take a 5 minute break to stretch and breathe, or simply relax your body so that you prepare your body for lunch in a peaceful environment.

2:00 PM   Drink a glass of water, juice, milk or other liquid and then *have lunch*.

2:45 PM   Rest at least 30 minutes to 1 hour to allow your body to fully digest the food.

4:00 PM   Start your afternoon training which might include going to the gym or simply resting if your morning training was enough.

5:00 PM   Complete abdominal exercises.

6:30 PM   Drink a glass of water, milk, or juice before *having dinner*. Remember to eat only foods explained in the nutrition plan in the first chapter.

8:30 PM   Eat a snack if your still hungry. Make sure to eat small quantities. <u>Remember that after dark you do not eat any carbs, fruits or foods that contain either one.</u>

10:00 PM   You should drink at least one glass of water before going to *sleep even if you sleep earlier or later than the time provided*.

Note:

You can adjust the schedule and the exercises as long as all the steps are completed and are in order. Also, make sure you stay within the 3 hour time difference between meals and drink a minimum of 6 – 8 glasses of water before the end of the day.

Improving the quality of events in your life and daily schedule will help you lose weight even while you are sleeping as your metabolism will accelerate at a faster rate and will move its way to your sleeping hours.

Saturday

For Saturday's schedule we are simply going to replace the time at work with time at home, entertainment, or doing some chores. Saturday would look something like this:

7:00 AM   Drink one glass of water when you *wake up*.

7:15 AM   Do a 5 minute morning stretch to get your muscles relaxed and ready for the day ahead.

8:00 AM   Drink a glass of water, milk, or juice and then *eat breakfast*. Base your breakfast on the diet plan explained in chapter 1.

8:30 AM   Train as you normally would on a weekday.

10:00 AM   Drink one glass of water.

11:00 AM	Eat a fruit along with a multigrain bar (or another snack based on the list provided in chapter 1.). You can add or replace it with a yogurt or slices of a protein (turkey, ham, roast beef, fish, poultry, etc.).
11:10 AM	After having your snack make sure to take a 5 minute break to stretch and breathe, or simply relax your body so that you prepare your body for lunch in a peaceful environment.
2:00 PM	Drink a glass of water, juice, milk or other liquid and then *have lunch*.
2:45 PM	Rest
5:30 PM	Drink a glass of water, milk, or juice before *having dinner*. Remember to eat only foods in

the nutrition guide provided at the beginning of this book.

8:30 PM   Eat a small meal and include a glass of water with this meal.

10:00 PM   Drink a glass of water before going to *sleep*.

CHAPTER 3

HOW TO GET IN SHAPE

24 HOURS A DAY

Accelerating your metabolism to enhance performance

What you do if I told you that you could get in shape 24 hours a day? Sound impossible? Let me tell you how to do it through a very simple process that might surprise you in a sense because of its simplicity but first we will focus on the three main components of staying in shape and losing weight. They are: Patience, repetition, and focus.

Patience

It takes time to gain weight. Some people spend a year or more increasing their weight without ever controlling it. Dropping all that weight that has taken so long to accumulate takes time if you want lasting results. Let me repeat that one more time because it's a difficult concept to understand. It takes time to drop all the weight you have accumulated over the years. If you want quick results just work smarter and improve your nutrition. If you lose weight fast, be sure that it will come back just as fast if you don't continue to do what you did to drop it. *Don't fall for the easy way out* because it won't last and you'll be right back where you started. Be patient as small decreases in weight are more valuable in the long run than large ones that come right back. Your body will gradually adjust to the exercise routines and the nutritional plan. That means you will be building off your new results each time. Just be patient.

Over time your body weight works like a seesaw.

Your weight will increase as time goes by if you don't take the necessary steps to maintain it at a healthy level and it will decrease as time goes by if you work hard to control it. Maintaining your body weight is a matter of balance between nutrition and exercise.

Repetition

Changing your lifestyle takes time and it takes permanent decisions. If you decide to start working out but find yourself training once a week or every other week, then you obviously know what type of results you will have. You've got to be consistent. Also, you need to be repetitive in what you, from the first day of the month until the last day of the month. It sounds like a lot of work, but you have to realize that you already do a lot of things in a consistent manner that you might not have noticed. Do you eat at least three times a day, every day of every month of the year? <u>Do you watch TV at least an hour every day of every month?</u> Do you change your clothes every day of every month of the year? And do you take a shower every day of every month of the year? If you answered "yes" to these questions, it means you do a lot of things in a consistent way. I bet a lot of people never even realize they do all these things every day. It's definitely something you should use to your advantage, by simply adding some exercises and an effective diet plan to these everyday activities.

There are "quick fixes" that can get you where you want to be but most of the time they'll have some sort of side effect or health risk involved. That's not what this book is about. You're working on obtaining <u>long term results that will last</u> and that will eventually become a part of your life. That's why it's important to stick to these exercises and allow them to become a part of your daily life.

The most important thing is to be consistent if you want long term results so stay focused on getting there.

Focus

Focus is the art of being able to concentrate on something for a determined period of time. That's what I want you to do with your new exercise routine and dietary plan. Stay focused no matter what. Stay focused on the objective at hand. Stay focused on your new lifestyle. Work at it every day because it's your life and it's up to you and no one else to make it better.

How to get in shape 24 hours a day

We spoke about increasing your RMR in the last chapter but now let's go into more detail.

Step 1: Start doing more exercise, preferably the exercises that involve increasing the amount of muscle in your body. Your body will to have to regenerate muscle tissue during the night time and this will contribute towards burning more energy. By doing this, you will lose weight and get fitter during the entire day!

Step 2: Follow the nutritional instructions described in chapter 1. Eating better and at scheduled times will change the short and long term effects your body and mind will have over time by reducing fat and simple sugar intake. This will help you to have a better defense mechanism that in turn will prevent you from getting sick or injured. It will boost your energy levels as well as help prevent future health problems such as obesity and heart disease. This is just to name a few of the most common ailments affecting our society today.

Step 3: Non-athletes need to drink a minimum of 6 to 8 glasses of water during the day, <u>especially one glass upon waking up and one before going to sleep.</u> As an athlete you should drink 6-10 glasses of water.

The Right Way to Drink Water

Water intake before the exercise, during the exercise and after the exercise should be properly planned.

A) Before training or competition consume 14-18 ounces of water two hours before any exercise. The two hour gap is enough to fully hydrate the body and leave enough time for excess water to come out of the system.

Take 5-7 ounces of water just 15 minutes before training.

B) During training or competition an athlete must constantly keep hydrating the body every 20-25 minutes with 5-10 ounces of water. Sports drinks are good sources of sodium which needs to be replenished in competition but should be mixed with some water to dilute the high sugar content they usually have to make them taste good.

Athletes who perspire excessively should consume 1.5 g of sodium and 2.3 g of chloride each day (or 3.8 g of salt) to replace the amount lost through perspiration. The maximum amount should not exceed 5.8 g of salt each day (2.3 g of sodium). Consult with your doctor if you have any of these medical conditions: elevated blood pressure, coronary heart disease, diabetes, and kidney disease, etc. These athletes should avoid consuming salt at the upper level. Endurance athletes and other individuals who are involved in strenuous activities are allowed to consume more sodium to offset sweat losses. The carbonates in the sports drinks also help the muscles perform better. Athletes should also have an adequate intake of 4.7 g of potassium per day to blunt the effects of salt, lower blood pressure, and reduce the risk of kidney stones and bone loss. Athletes should also eat foods rich in potassium such as bananas and prunes.

C) After training or competition an athlete should replace all lost fluids by drinking approximately 20 ounces of fluid for every pound of weight lost.

Step 4: Sleep at least 5 hours but no more than 10 per day and take power naps during the day if you feel you need to get more rest. Sleeping allows your body to recover from the wear and tear you experience every day. It's also a good time for your body to recover so that you can continue training the following day. Sleeping is an excellent way to relieve your body and mind of any excess stress that has accumulated during the day. Sleeping is important so make sure you get adequate hours of sleep every night.

Step 5: Working your cardiovascular endurance is a great way to accelerate your metabolism which will also strengthen your heart. Make sure you do as much aerobic exercise as possible without getting injured. Besides static exercises and stretching, aerobic exercises will provide you with one of the most important tools you can have towards having a higher resting metabolic rate which we talked about in the last chapter. Some good aerobic exercises you can do to cross train are: running, swimming, jumping, roller-blading, skiing, rowing, karate, and playing sports that require any combination of these. A good cardiovascular exercise you can do after lunch is walk up and down stairs at a slow pace and at a low intensity level. If you work or live in a building that has stairs, make sure you take advantage of this. A building with two floors would be sufficient since you can go up and down the same steps. Make sure you do this for at least 5 minutes to make it worthwhile. After eating, always try to do some form of low-intensity aerobic exercise besides walking up and down stairs. This might be one of the most important changes you make towards improving your overall health and fitness.

Our goal in this chapter is to naturally accelerate your metabolism by staying as active as possible during most of the day which will increase your RMR. A faster metabolism helps your body stay lean and fit but you want to make sure you do this naturally (without the use of artificial substances) and gradually so that these changes are easily maintained in months and years to come.

A SIMPLE EXPLANATION ON LOSING, GAINING, AND MAINTAINING BODY WEIGHT

Losing, gaining, and maintaining weight is all about simple math. If you consume 1 unit of food and exercise 1 unit, you will have a simple mathematical equation that looks like this:

$$1 - 1 = 0$$

Meaning, if you exercise the same amount you eat (unit wise) you should gain little or no weight.

Now, if you consume 1 unit of food and exercise "0" units, you will have an equation that looks like this:

$$1 - 0 = 1$$

Meaning, you will have gained "1" unit of weight. (I use the term "unit" to simplify things but it refers to the amount of weight.) This simply means that every day that you eat and don't exercise, you gain weight because you have a surplus.

Last, if you consume "1" unit of food and exercise "2" units, you will have an equation that will look like this:

$$1 - 2 = -1$$

Meaning, you have lost one unit of weight.

Important note: Not consuming any units of food (not eating) is not an option because this will create more harm than good. Instead of achieving your goals you will be delaying them and even causing irreversible health problems. You need food to survive. It is a basic necessity of life.

WHAT DOES THIS ALL MEAN?

The amount and quality of exercise you do will determine if you lose, gain, or maintain weight. Depending on what your goals are, this can actually make your life healthier. Just make sure to follow a nutritional plan that is right for you and your lifestyle. Refer to chapter 1 for more information on what you should be eating and how much of it. Warning! Do not go to extremes. Some people get sick by going on extreme diets that can ultimately create more harm than benefit. Below are some examples of extremes you want to avoid:

EXAMPLE 1

By eating simple sugars and fats, and NOT consuming food with nutritional value will reduce your potential performance outcome and will lower your quality of health in years to come. A balanced diet is necessary to stay fit. Even though this would not be considered an extreme diet it is still suggested that you stay away from prepackaged and canned foods, as well as foods with high fat content not derived from natural sources. Natural sources of fat would be avocado, nuts, olive oil, etc. and these are good for you but in the right proportions.

EXAMPLE 2

If you are an athlete that does a lot of cardio exercise and don't consume any carbohydrates such as bread, rice, and pasta. It can seriously affect your performance as well as your wellbeing. Cutting carbs completely out of your diet might not be a wise decision. If this is the case, you should consume some form of carbohydrate during the day to maintain the right energy reserves your body needs. You can still control your body weight but you have to consume at least a minimum of nutrients from a variety of food groups and this includes carbohydrates.

EXAMPLE 3

Eating a lot and not exercising. This is what this book focuses on preventing. This book will definitely help you to get fitter and improve the shape of your body into the body you've always wanted. Make it a priority to balance your nutritional life with everyday cardiovascular training.

EXAMPLE 4

Not sleeping enough can severely affect your mental and physical condition during training and competition. Sleeping allows you to recover and perform better in all aspects of your life. Take the necessary steps to control the amount and quality of your sleep.

CHAPTER 4

BETTER SWIMMING PERFORMANCE THROUGH ANTIOXIDANTS

Change your nutritional lifestyle now to get long term results and faster recovery times

A number of elements in our body such as sunlight and pollution in our environment produce oxidation leading to the production of dangerous chemical compounds called free radicals. Free radicals can lead to serious cellular damage, which is the common pathway for cancer, ageing, and a variety of other diseases. Free radicals are highly reactive and pose a major threat by reacting with cell membranes in chain reactions leading to the death of the cells. Antioxidants are molecules that can help in destroying the free radicals so that the body can be free from the dangers associated with the free radicals. Moreover, athletes should have a keen interest in them because of health concerns and the prospect of enhanced performance and/or recovery after exercise. The way antioxidants work is that they can react with the free radicals and shut down the chain reaction leading to the death of the DNA cells and thus save them.

The main sources of antioxidants are:

1. Vitamin E: It is an antioxidant and helps protect cells from damage. It is also important for the health of red blood cells. Vitamin E is found in many foods such as vegetable oils, nuts, and leafy green vegetables. Avocados, wheat germ, and whole grains are also good sources of this vitamin.

2. Beta-carotene: It is a precursor to vitamin A (retinol) and is present in liver, egg yolk, milk, butter, spinach, carrots, tomatoes, and grains.

3. Vitamin C: It is needed to form collagen, a tissue that helps in holding cells together. It is essential for healthy bones, teeth, gums, and blood vessels. It helps the body absorb iron and calcium, aids in wound healing, and contributes to brain function. You will find high levels of vitamin C in red berries, kiwifruit, red and green bell peppers, tomatoes, broccoli, spinach, and juices made from guava, grapefruit,   and   orange.

4. Selenium: It is a trace element and is also an important antioxidant.

Some Popular Antioxidants are Mentioned Below:

Strengthening our immune system will help you absorb antioxidants and protect you from free radicals which can be done through exercise. That's why a combination of cardiovascular and weight training in combination with added antioxidants in your diet will improve you performance and allow you to have less low energy or sick days. By consuming more antioxidants your recovery phase will be faster which will allow you to compete sooner than normal.

Project the Right Image through a

Better Posture to Win More

Studies have shown that athletes who project a strong positive image are prone to being more successful and have a stronger immune system. Having a strong immune system will keep you healthier and prone to less injuries which equates to having the prospect of winning more simply because you can compete more often.

Definitive change from the caveman era to now is our posture. For some reason a lot of athletes look like they are back in the caveman era. Maybe some athletes have this hunched posture because they don't work on flexibility and back strengthening exercises or maybe because of lack of confidence. Whatever may be the reason, an athlete's posture says a lot about how they feel and what they project specially to their competition. Showing a lack of confidence to your competition will only motivate them to do better. To succeed more as an athlete start showing more confidence through a better posture even when you are not competing.

Most of us forget that as we get older our backs hunch even more and it becomes more difficult to stay straight. I would rather work on having a better posture now than later because later might never come. I forgot to mention that not standing up straight makes you look fatter as well. So if you want to start looking thinner, start standing up straight! For this and many other reasons, it's essential to focus on your posture.

It has often been overlooked by many but can help you get to a better figure faster than you can imagine. Did you know that by walking in a slouched position you are actually making your stomach muscles lazier and thus promoting that shape of abdominal muscles? Not a good habit to have. By walking straight you are actually working your abs.

Posture is a matter of habit

You must concentrate on maintaining a straight posture all the time. Focus on keeping a good posture when you walk, when you sit and when you stand. Posture is also very important when you eat because it helps food pass through your digestive system easier than if you were slouched. Chewing your food better can contribute to the reduction or better yet, prevention, of digestion or acid reflux related issues.

Also, *consider that no matter how hard you work and how good a body you may have, if you slouch, you just ruined the picture (the image of yourself and what you project to others) and made all that effort become almost unnoticed.* For this specific reason, I want to remind you how vital it is to concentrate, work on and make a habit of standing, sitting and walking with a straight posture.

Key points to having a better posture are:

1. Your Shoulders should be relaxed and below your neck height.
2. Your Chest should be out and shoulders back.
3. Your Head needs to be perpendicular to the ground. (Imagine drawing a straight line from your chin to the ground.)
4. Your Eyes should be focused on the horizon NOT on the ground.

CHAPTER 5

YOU ARE WHAT YOU EAT

Commit to improving your mind and body

Does that sound strange to you? "You are what you eat". It's a simple statement with a lot of meaning. What you do during the day or for a living determines what types of activities you physically and mentally do. You become a more active or sedentary person depending on how you spend your time and what you eat. This determines who you are at the end.

Changing your habits

Change your habits by changing your dietary, mental, and physical lifestyle. <u>This means being able to do the same things you already do but now replacing some foods with healthier and more</u>

organic ones. As time goes by you'll feel stronger, more flexible and full of energy because the nutrients you feed your body. *How do you go from eating junk food to healthy food?* This is basically obtained, through discipline and consistency. Use daily food schedule included in the first chapters of this book as guideline to get you there. With time you will be eating right every day and will become a habit. This should be one of your primary goals.

Making the best of your particular situation

Never feel bad about yourself. There's always some else in a worse situation. If you have a bad back and its hurts when you walk, then there's probably someone who can't walk at all so be thankful. If you have knee problems, instead of complaining be happy you have legs. These examples are a little drastic but to the point. If want to get started, you have to make sure you have no excuses so that you don't stop with any excuse. If your back hurts, swim. If your knees hurt, strengthen them or work on your upper body. If your shoulder hurts, work on your abdominals or legs. Learn to improvise.

Different climate

If you live in a place where the weather is terrible you don't really have to worry too much because most of these exercises can be done indoors as well. If it's hot outside then take advantage of the pool exercises. If it's cold outside do the indoor exercises. Just don't stay still

If you feel that having a better nutritional plan or diet is expensive

If this is your case try to find alternatives to the foods described in this book. Instead of going to a major supermarket, try going to a discount food store or food store that sells in bulk. If you plan on sticking to the diet you should have what you need for months to come so you might as well buy in bulk if it works to your advantage cost wise. Another way to economize is to find a training partner to work with you and who can share the costs of food, if that becomes the case. Never let money become the reason for not being in better shape or being healthy!

Remind yourself to train and stick with this nutritional plan

An easy way to remind yourself that you have to train and stick with the nutritional plan is to carry this book around. That way you have the exercises on hand at any time. Another great way to remind yourself that you need to train eat at the right times is to wear a watch with an alarm on it to remind you every hour or every three hours that you need to be taking care of yourself. If you get tired of your watch, I have another great way to remind yourself. Try placing your training shoes or clothes on the floor next to your bed or at the door. Every time you wake up or are simply walking to the door, you will see your shoes and will remember what you need to be doing. If you left your shoes and clothes at the door, you would know you should not be leaving the room until you are done with your training. You have to prepare to succeed and this is how you do it. Help yourself by doing these little things that make a big difference every day.

Remind yourself to resist distractions

Go to the refrigerator and take out all of the food that you should not be eating. Clean the entire refrigerator if need be. Organize the shelves so that you know what you are supposed to eat for breakfast, lunch, and dinner. Make it easy for yourself to eat what you know you should be eating. Keep only fresh food as you don't want to get sick. A lot of people have refrigerators full of food they stocked up months ago and haven't taken the time to throw out expired food. In the refrigerator, keep fruits and vegetables in Ziploc® bags and in lower compartments to make sure they last fresh for as long as possible. <u>Place your dietary plan on the outside of the refrigerator, in your room and in your office to keep you focused.</u>

Don't let others bring you down

You should become your best fan, cheering and pushing hard every day to stick to the diet and exercise plan. If you have others telling you that you won't last on the diet or that you won't continue doing the training routine, stay away from these people. If you can't stay away from these people, learn to separate the noise in what they say from what is actually valuable to you. You have radio and TV commercials as well as shows and some static. Do you focus on the static, the music or the commercials? The same thing will happen in life. You will always have someone who makes a comment just to impose their ideas or their negativity. Don't argue; instead find people who want to accomplish the same things you are trying to accomplish. Search for people who can help you stay focused and truly want you to be successful. Surround yourself with positive, uplifting, and motivated people. Even if others bring you down, show them you can and will make it through this diet. Prove to your kids that you can do anything you set your mind on no matter how difficult it may seem.

When you feel that you lack motivation, I want you to read this to yourself:

- ✓ I will complete my workout today.
- ✓ I will stick to my diet and will not deviate from it.
- ✓ I am the only one who can decide if I am successful or not.
- ✓ It is my responsibility to follow through on my training and diet.
- ✓ I can do it, therefore I will do it.
- ✓ I am the result of my actions.
- ✓ I believe in myself and in my potential.

By reading this to yourself you'll feel a lot better and it will show in your actions!

Write down 10 reasons why you believe you will be successful in completing this diet and exercise routine:

1.

2.

3.

4.

5.

6.

7.

8.

9.

10.

When you're having a bad day read what you just wrote above. Think about what was going through your mind when you wrote these 10 reasons and what you should be thinking right now. Everyone has good and bad days. The key is to get past the bad days in the best possible way so that the good days are that much better. Remember, the results you have today will be the product of efforts made in days before.

Write down 5 physical changes you want to see in your body once completing this diet and exercise routine:

1.

2.

3.

4.

5.

Write down 5 mental or emotional changes you want to reach upon completing this diet and exercise routine: (ex. I want to be more positive, I want to feel happier about myself and my appearance, I want to have less stress in my life, I want to feel I have more energy every day, etc.)

1.

2.

3.

4.

5.

Write down 10 goals you have for yourself regarding exercise, nutrition, and your life in general. Completing this diet and exercise plan should be a part of your general goals:

1.

2.

3.

4.

5.

6.

7.

8.

9.

10.

CHAPTER 6

INCREASE YOUR PROTEIN WITH HOMEMADE MEAL RECIPES FOR SWIMMING

Taking the next step to see results

The only way to see results is to actually get started and the best way to do this is by making a list of what you need to buy at the grocery store and then bringing those items home. Replace all current unhealthy foods with as many ingredients and foods that you see in the recipes included below. If your refrigerator only has foods that you should be eating, it will be easier for you to stay on track. Repeat this process every time you are running out of food so that you don't eat out as much or become tempted to eat at fast food restaurants.

HOMEMADE PROTEIN MEALS

1. Chicken wraps

Ingredients:

1 pound of chicken breast, boneless and skinless

2 cups of chicken broth

1 cup of Greek yogurt

1 cup of fresh parsley, chopped

½ tsp of sea salt

¼ tsp of ground pepper

4 cups of chopped lettuce

1 cup of diced tomato

½ cup of onion, sliced

1 package of tortillas (low carb, whole wheat)

Preparation:

Combine chicken broth and chicken meat in a sauce pan over medium heat. Cover the sauce pan and allow it to boil. Cook for another 10-15 over medium-low heat. Remove from heat and drain. Let it stand for a while. Chop the meat into bite size pieces.

Meanwhile, in a large bowl, combine Greek yogurt, chicken meat, parsley, salt and pepper. Mix gently until the chicken is well coated. Spread this mixture over tortillas and top with lettuce, tomato and onion. Roll and serve.

Nutritional values for one tortilla:

Carbohydrates 14.5 g

Sugar 2.5g

Protein 21.5 g

Total fat 5g

Sodium 568.2 mg

Potassium 83.2mg

Calcium 31mg

Iron 9mg

Vitamins (vitamin A; B-6; B-12; C; D; D2; D3; K; Riboflavin; Niacin; Thiamin; K)

Calories 167

2. Italian pasta

Ingredients:

1 cup of whole grain pasta

2 cups of shrimps

1 cup of red peppers, chopped

1 tbsp of Parmesan cheese

4 tbsp of Greek yogurt

Preparation:

Use package directions to boil pasta. Drain well and let it stand.

Meanwhile, combine red peppers, Parmesan cheese and Greek yogurt in a saucepan. Let it melt over a medium temperature and add shrimps. Stir fry for 5 minutes.

Pour the shrimp sauce over pasta and serve warm.

Nutritional values per 100g:

Carbohydrates 22g

Sugar 7g

Protein 23.2 g

Total fat 6.3g

Sodium 531.5 mg

Potassium 112.1mg

Calcium 28mg

Iron 8.2mg

Vitamins (vitamin A; B-6; B-12; C; D; D2; D3; K;
Riboflavin; Niacin; Thiamin; K)

Calories 212

3. Cilantro garlic burgers topped with parmesan

Ingredients:

2 cans of lentils, drained

3 cloves of garlic, minced

½ cup of breadcrumbs

¼ cup of parmesan cheese (freshly grated is best, but whatever you got will work)

1 egg, beaten

2 cups of water

½ cup of flour

salt and pepper to taste

Preparation:

In a medium size bowl, mash lentils with folk then mix with garlic, breadcrumbs and cheese. Form into patties; set aside. Whisk egg and water in bowl; flour and salt & pepper in another bowl. Coat each patty gently with flour mixture, dip into egg, then coat again with flour. Over medium-high heat in a large skillet, heat oil. Fry the burgers until lightly brown, about 2-3 minutes each side.

Serve on warm bread or in a pita with cilantro, yogurt, onion, tomatoes and whatever else you like – but this is optional!

Nutritional values per 100g:

Carbohydrates 16.1g

Sugar 4.5g

Protein 19.8g

Total fat 6.7g

Sodium 511mg

Potassium 96.1mg

Calcium 27mg

Iron 8.9mg

Vitamins (vitamin A; B-6; B-12; C; D; D2; D3; K; Riboflavin; Niacin; Thiamin; K)

Calories 195

4. Potato and cheese

Ingredients:

3 medium potatoes

½ cup of cottage cheese

¼ cup of cheddar cheese

¼ cup of organic tomato puree

¼ cup parsley, chopped

Directions

Preheat the oven to 350 degrees. Wash and peel the potatoes. Cut each potato into 2 slices and bake for 30 minutes. Remove from the oven.

Combine cottage and cheddar cheese in a bowl and spread over potato slices. Allow it to melt slightly. Top with tomato puree and chopped parsley. Serve immediately.

Nutritional values per 100g:

Carbohydrates 21.8g

Sugar 9.3g

Protein 21g

Total fat 7g

Sodium 312 mg

Potassium 61mg

Calcium 19.7mg

Iron 5mg

Vitamins (vitamin A; B-6; B-12; C; D; D2; D3; K; Riboflavin; Niacin; Thiamin; K)

Calories 154

5. Curry lentils

Ingredients:

1 cup of lentils

1 cup of low fat cream

4 cups of water

¼ tsp of salt

½ teaspoon of coriander powder

½ teaspoon of cayenne pepper

¼ tsp of turmeric powder

1 tsp of ground cumin

1 small to medium sized onion (chopped)

2 tbsp of butter

1 tbsp of chinese parsley (for garnishing)

Preparation:

Soak lentils in cool water for 1 hour to overnight, this will make the cooking process easier and less time consuming (but can be skipped). Before cooking rinse lentils and drain the excess water thoroughly.

Pour water in a large saucepan and bring to boil, then turn the heat to medium-low. In hot water add lentils, garlic, salt, coriander, pepper, and turmeric powder. Cover and leave until lentils are tender. This process will take about 30 minutes to 1 hour. You can add more water if necessary.

When lentils are soft and cooked, melt the butter in a pot over low to medium heat. Stir chopped onion until they turn golden brown, then add cumin, and fry about a minute on a low temperature. Stir constantly.

Stir the onions and butter into the lentils; cook on low heat for another 5 to 8 minutes. Add low fat cream and allow it to melt.

Garnish with chopped parsley and serve.

Nutritional values per 100g:

Carbohydrates 18.1g

Sugar 6.1g

Protein 17.5g

Total fat 3g

Sodium 112mg

Potassium 43.3mg

Calcium 19mg

Iron 6mg

Vitamins (vitamin A; B-6; B-12; C; D; D2; D3; K;
Riboflavin; Niacin; Thiamin; K)

Calories 97

6. Winter chicken surprise

Ingredients:

1 pound of boneless chicken, chopped

1 2/3 cups of chicken broth

2/4 cup of chopped onions

½ cup of brown rice

½ cup of cottage cheese

3 tbsp of Greek yogurt

¼ tsp of salt

½ tsp of basil

¼ tsp of oregano

¼ tsp of thyme, crushed

1/8 tsp of garlic powder

1/8 tsp of pepper

½ cup of cheese shredded

Preparation:

Combine the chicken and onions into a skillet and cook between medium to high heat until chicken is cooked. This should take about 20-30 minutes.

Place chicken and onions into a large bowl and then add chicken broth, uncooked brown rice, basil, salt, oregano, thyme, garlic powder, pepper and cottage cheese. Mix up until everything is thoroughly combined.

Place the mixture into an ungreased 1½ quart casserole dish with a tight fitting lid.

Preheat oven to 250 degrees. Bake covered for about 30 minutes, or until rice is done, stirring it several times during cooking.

Uncover the casserole dish and top with Greek yogurt.

Bake uncovered for about five more minutes until yogurt is completely melted. Garnish with parsley before serving.

Nutritional values per 100g:

Carbohydrates 16.1g

Sugar 2.5g

Protein 23.5 g

Total fat 5g

Sodium 567.1 mg

Potassium 84.2mg

Calcium 33mg

Iron 9.4mg

Vitamins (vitamin A; B-6; B-12; C; D; D2; D3; K; Riboflavin; Niacin; Thiamin; K)

Calories 198

7. Mushroom sliders

Ingredients:

1 sweet potato

1 cup of fresh button mushrooms

1 cup of cottage cheese

3 egg whites

¾ cup of chia seeds

¾ of a cup of long grain rice

¾ of a cup of bread crumbs

1 tsp of tarragon

1 tsp of parsley

1 tsp of garlic powder

1 cup of chopped spinach

Preparation:

Pour 1 cup of water in a small saucepan. Bring it to boil and cook rice until it's slightly sticky. This should take about 10 minutes. At the same time, cook chia seeds until soft in a separate pot. Finely chop mushrooms . Thoroughly rinse spinach. Mix all the ingredients together in a large bowl . Put the bowl into the fridge to chill for 15 to 30 minutes. Take mixture out of the fridge and form into patties. Make sure cooking surfaces are cleaned and greased before adding patties to prevent them from sticking. Fry each piece on a medium temperature for about 5 minutes on both side.

Nutritional values per 100g:

Carbohydrates 19g

Sugar 7.5g

Protein 22g

Total fat 5.8g

Sodium 532 mg

Potassium 83mg

Calcium 31.3mg

Iron 7mg

Vitamins (vitamin A; B-6; B-12; C; D; D2; D3; K; Riboflavin; Niacin; Thiamin; K)

Calories 186

8. Chia seeds – indian way

Ingredients:

1 cup of chia seeds

1 cup of low fat cream

2 cloves of garlic, chopped

1 tsp of ground ginger

¼ tsp of salt

2 small chili peppers

1 small onion, chopped

Preparation:

Use 3 cups of water and bring it to boil. Put chia seeds in it and cook it for 30 minutes on a low temperature. When tender, add spices and mix well. Cook for about 5-10 minutes on a low temperature, stirring constantly. Top with low fat cream.

Nutritional values per 100g:

Carbohydrates 12.1g

Sugar 4.5g

Protein 15 g

Total fat 4g

Sodium 263.mg

Potassium 81 mg

Calcium 11mg

Iron 3mg

Vitamins (vitamin A; B-6; B-12; C; D; D2; D3; K;
Riboflavin; Niacin; Thiamin; K)

Calories 111

9. Chicken chops

Ingredients:

1 cup of chicken fillets, chopped

3 tbsp of olive oil

2 tbsp of ginger, freshly chopped

2 garlic cloves, minced

5 scallions, diced

1 tbsp of curry powder

4 carrots, chopped

4 cups of chicken broth

salt to taste

ground pepper to taste

lime

Preparation:

Heat the oil over medium heat in a saucepan. Add in and saute the garlic scallions and ginger until soft. Add in the remaining ingredients, stir and bring to boiling. Reduce the heat to low, cover and let it simmer for about 20 minutes so the meat becomes tender. Pour into bowls and serve.

Nutritional values per 100g:

Carbohydrates 13g

Sugar 5.5g

Protein 19.3 g

Total fat 4g

Sodium 363.2 mg

Potassium 82.1mg

Calcium 21mg

Iron 4.3mg

Vitamins (vitamin A; B-6; B-12; C; D; D2; D3; K; Riboflavin; Niacin; Thiamin; K)

Calories 134

10. Lentil burgers

Ingredients:

1 clove of garlic, peeled

½ tsp salt

1 cup of chopped walnuts

¼ tsp of black pepper, finely grounded

2 cups of rinsed lentils

2 tsp of canola oil

2 pieces of wheat bread torn into bite sized pieces

4 wheat burger buns

1 cup of chopped lettuce, red onions and tomatoes

Preparation:

Chop up the garlic clove as finely as possible. Add in the other spices (salt and pepper) to the garlic mash and mix well. Next put the nuts into a food processor and finely chop them as well before adding them to the garlic mash. Add the pieces of bread next and then finally, the lentils. Mix well, either by hand or food processor (I recommend the food processor) until the mass of ingredients come together in a mass. Remove mix and patty out four burgers from it. You are now ready to cook these beauties! Heat up the oil in a skillet set on medium heat. Add the patties and cook until each one is nicely browned on both sides.This should take no more than six minutes to complete.Put those patties on a bun, add the fixings and you have yourself a delicious and healthy protein lunch!

Nutritional values per 100g:

Carbohydrates 25g

Sugar 13.2g

Protein 26.3 g

Total fat 11g

Sodium 575 mg

Potassium 92mg

Calcium 28mg

Iron 9.7mg

Vitamins (vitamin A; B-6; B-12; C; D; D2; D3; K; Riboflavin; Niacin; Thiamin; K)

Calories 194

11. Chickpea & chili soup

Ingredients:

2 tsp of cumin seeds

½ cup of chili flakes

½ cup of lentils

1 tbsp of olive oil

1 red onion , chopped

3 cups of vegetable stock

1 cup of can tomatoes, whole or chopped

½ cup of chickpeas

small bunch of coriander, roughly chopped

4 tbsp of Greek yogurt, for serving

Preparation:

Heat a large saucepan and dry-fry the cumin seeds and chili flakes for 1 minute or until they start to jump around the pan and release their aromas. Add the oil and onion, and cook for 5 minutes. Stir in the lentils, stock and tomatoes, then bring to the boil. Simmer for 15 minutes until the lentils have softened.

Mix the soup with a stick blender or in a food processor until it is a rough purée, pour back into the pan and add the chickpeas. Heat gently, season well and stir in the coriander. Finish with a dollop of yogurt and coriander leaves.

Nutritional values per 100g:

Carbohydrates 18g

Sugar 9.8g

Protein 21g

Total fat 7g

Sodium 529mg

Potassium 63.1mg

Calcium 21mg

Iron 8.9mg

Vitamins (vitamin A; B-6; B-12; C; D; D2; D3; K; Riboflavin; Niacin; Thiamin; K)

Calories 120

12. Quinoa & Shrimp Paella

Ingredients:

1 pound of frozen shrimps, cleaned

1 cup of dry quinoa

2 cups of chicken broth

1 medium onion, diced

2 cloves of garlic, minced

1 tbsp of olive oil

1 bay leaf

½ tsp of red pepper, ground

½ tsp of green pepper, ground

½ tsp of black pepper, ground

¼ tsp of sea salt

½ cup of chopped dry tomatoes

1 cup of green peas

1 tsp of organic seafood seasoning

Preparation:

Use package instructions to prepare quinoa.
Meanwhile, wash and drain shrimps. Sprinkle
them with a pinch of salt and leave in the
refrigerator.

In a large saucepan, heat the olive oil over a
medium temperature. Add onions and stir well.
Fry for about 5 minutes. Add garlic and saute for 1
minute. Now add quinoa, chicken broth and
spices. Cover and allow it to boil. Reduce heat and
continue cooking for another 10-15 minutes. You
don't want any liquid left.

Remove from heat and add dry tomatoes, peas
and shrimps. Cover and allow it to stand for about
5 minutes before serving.

Nutritional values per 1 cup:

Carbohydrates 31g

Sugar 3.8g

Protein 27g

Total fat 6g

Sodium 412mg

Potassium 623mg

Calcium 171.7mg

Iron 0.83mg

Vitamins (Vitamin C total ascorbic acid; B-6; B-12; Folate-DFE; A-RAE; A-IU; E-alpha-tocopherol; D; D-D2+D3; Thianin; Niacin)

Calories 283

13. British chia seeds

Ingredients:

2 cups of chia seeds

2 tbs Worcestershire Sauce

1 tsp Malt vinegar

2 tsp of salt

2 cups of water

Preparation:

It is best to soak the seeds for 8-12 hours, but if you can't then cook them in water for 35 - 45 minutes until they start to soften.

When chia seeds start to soften, add other ingredients. Cook until seeds are soft enough that they will mash easily with a large spoon.

Make sure there is a small amount of liquid in the mixture until the very end of the cooking process. It's best to add half a cup of water at a time and stir frequently.

Nutritional values per 100g:

Carbohydrates 12g

Sugar 2 g

Protein 11g

Total fat 3.4g

Sodium 166.9 mg

Potassium 73.1mg

Calcium 21mg

Iron 5.1mg

Vitamins (vitamin A; B-6; B-12; C; D; D2; D3; K; Riboflavin; Niacin; Thiamin; K)

Calories 146

14. Barbecue peas

Ingredients:

2 cups of canned peas, washed and rinsed

5 cups of water

½ cup of non fat yogurt

½ cup of Greek yogurt

2 tbsp of brown sugar

1 tbsp of vinegar

1 tsp of mustard

1 tsp of Worcestershire sauce

2 tsp of tomato sauce

1 small chopped onion

Preparation:

Preheat your oven at 350 degrees. Pour peas in water, and bring it to boil. Let it boil for 30 minutes, or until tender. Make sure that they remain whole. Add all the ingredients to the boiled and tender peas, and stir the mixture to combine them well. Pour the peas in a baking dish an and bake for 45 minutes. Top with Greek yogurt.

Nutritional values per 100g:

Carbohydrates 22.3g

Sugar 6.1g

Protein 23.1 g

Total fat 6g

Sodium 428.1 mg

Potassium 73.2mg

Calcium 33mg

Iron 5mg

Vitamins (vitamin A; B-6; B-12; C; D; D2; D3; K; Riboflavin; Niacin; Thiamin; K)

Calories 167.5

15. Buckwheat pasta with mozzarella

Ingredients:

1 small pack of buckwheat pasta

½ cup of chia seeds powder

1 small can of sugar-free tomato sauce

1 small mozzarella

1 tsp of rosemary

olive oil

salt

Preparation:

Use package instructions to cook pasta. Wash it and drain. Chop mozzarella into small pieces and mix with tomato sauce. Add chia seeds powder to this mixture. Cook this sauce for about 10 minutes, stirring constantly. Add rosemary, olive oil and salt. Cook for another 4-5 minutes and pour over pasta.

Nutritional values per 100g:

Carbohydrates 20.1g

Sugar 8.5g

Protein 21.3 g

Total fat 7g

Sodium 268mg

Potassium 73.3mg

Calcium 22mg

Iron 5mg

Vitamins (vitamin A; B-6; B-12; C; D; D2; D3; K; Riboflavin; Niacin; Thiamin; K)

Calories 160

16. Turkey with vegetables

Ingredients:

1 pound of turkey, skinless and boneless

1 bunch of spinach

1 cup of chopped broccoli

¼ tsp of sea salt

¼ tsp of red pepper

Preparation:

Wash and cut turkey into bite size pieces. Put it in a large saucepan and add water to cover the meat. Bring it to boil over a high temperature. Cook until the meat is tender. Reduce the heat, add spinach and broccoli. Stir well and cook for another 15 minutes on a very low temperature. Add spices and serve warm.

Nutritional values per 100g:

Carbohydrates 10g

Sugar 2.4g

Protein 17.5 g

Total fat 4.8g

Sodium 161.4 mg

Potassium 31.5mg

Calcium 11mg

Iron 5.9mg

Vitamins (vitamin A; B-6; B-12; C; D; D2; D3; K; Riboflavin; Niacin; Thiamin; K)

Calories 112

17. Spinach ravioli

Ingredients:

3 cups of whole grain flour

2 cups of water

3 eggs

3 egg whites

6 tablespoons of olive oil

2 cups of spinach, chopped

1 cup of cottage cheese

1 cup of low fat yogurt

¼ tsp of salt

¼ tsp of pepper

Preparation:

In a large bowl, combine flour, water, eggs, egg whites, olive oil and a pinch of salt. You want to make a smooth dough. Cover and let it stand in a warm place for about 30 minutes.

Briefly boil spinach in salted water, drain and cut. Combine with cottage cheese, yogurt, salt and pepper.

Roll the dough thinly, cut out circles using molds and put in each hemisphere spoon of stuffing. Replace the second part of dough and press the edges with a fork so that the stuffing does not fall off.

Cook ravioli in boiling water to which you have added a little salt and olive oil. It should take about 15 minutes. Remove from the saucepan, drain and serve.

Nutritional values per 100g:

Carbohydrates 21.7g

Sugar 9.5g

Protein 28 g

Total fat 5g

Sodium 571.3 mg

Potassium 92.3mg

Calcium 40mg

Iron 9.8mg

Vitamins (vitamin A; B-6; B-12; C; D; D2; D3; K; Riboflavin; Niacin; Thiamin; K)

Calories 181

18. Grilled veal steak with fresh vegetables

Ingredients:

1 thick steak

1 medium carrot

1 bunch of lettuce

1 small tomato

1 small onion

2 tsp of Greek yogurt

1 cup of low fat cream

2 pickles

¼ tsp of salt

1/8 tsp of pepper

2 tbsp of olive oil

Preparation:

Wash and pat dry the steak with a kitchen paper. Cut into bite sizes and set aside. Heat up the olive oil over a medium temperature and fry the meat for about 15 minutes, stirring constantly. Remove from the heat and let it stand.

Wash and cut vegetables into small pieces. Combine with Greek yogurt and low fat cream. Season with salt and pepper and add meat in it.

Serve cold.

Nutritional values per 100g:

Carbohydrates 22.3g

Sugar 6.2g

Protein 23 g

Total fat 7g

Sodium 382.6 mg

Potassium 52mg

Calcium 21mg

Iron 5mg

Vitamins (vitamin A; B-6; B-12; C; D; D2; D3; K;
Riboflavin; Niacin; Thiamin; K)

Calories 175

19. Grilled salmon

Ingredients:

4 thick salmon fillets

2 tbsp of fresh lemon juice

¼ cup of fresh orange juice

¼ cup of low fat cream sauce

½ cup of chopped onions

1 tsp of dried parsley

1 tsp of ground garlic

cooking spray

Preparation:

In a large bowl, combine lemon juice, orange juice, low fat cream sauce, onions, parsley and garlic. Mix well to make a marinade. Add salmon fillets. Cover a bowl with a tight lid and leave in the refrigerator for about an hour.

Prepare a grill pan and sprinkle with cooking spray. Heat up over a high temperature and add salmon fillets. Fry for about 5 minutes on each side. You can add some more marinade while frying. Serve immediately.

Nutritional values per 100g:

Carbohydrates 17.2g

Sugar 3.5g

Protein 21.5 g

Total fat 5g

Sodium 528.1 mg

Potassium 84.1mg

Calcium 30mg

Iron 9mg

Vitamins (vitamin A; B-6; B-12; C; D; D2; D3; K; Riboflavin; Niacin; Thiamin; K)

Calories 171

20. Bean and mushroom mix

Ingredients:

2 cups of button mushrooms, sliced

1 cup of canned green beans, cooked

½ cup of onions, chopped

1 tbsp of fresh celery, chopped

¼ cup of apple vinegar

4 tbsp of sea salt

5 tbsp of extra virgin olive oil

1/3 cup of toasted almonds

1/3 cup of sliced dried figs

Preparation:

In a medium sized bowl, combine the onions with apple vinegar and let it stand for about 10-15 minutes. Add salt and 2 tbsp of olive oil.

Meanwhile, heat up the olive oil in a large saucepan and add the mushrooms. Cook for few minutes, stirring constantly. Remove from the heat when the mushrooms release their water. Add the beans, celery, figs and almonds to the saucepan. Mix well with mushrooms. Fry for several more minutes and remove from heat.

Pour the onion marinade on top and serve.

Nutritional values per 100g:

Carbohydrates 22.7g

Sugar 7.1g

Protein 19g

Total fat 7.4g

Sodium 570 mg

Potassium 71.2mg

Calcium 35.3mg

Iron 8mg

Vitamins (vitamin A; B-6; B-12; C; D; D2; D3; K; Riboflavin; Niacin; Thiamin; K)

Calories 167

21. Roasted lentils:

Ingredients:

½ cups of uncooked lentils

1 tbsp of salt

2 tbsp of olive oil

1 tsp of pepper

1 tsp of red chili powder

1 tsp of cinnamon powder

Preparation:

First you want to cook lentils. Pour about 2 cups of water in a saucepan and bring it to boil. Add lentils and boil for about 15-20 minutes, until soft from inside and still hold their shape. Remove from the heat and rinse well with cold water. Drain your chia seeds and set aside.

Preheat the oven to 300 degrees. In a large bowl, coat the lentils with salt, olive oil, pepper, red chili powder and cinnamon. Spread the lentils over a medium sized baking dish and bake for about 20 minutes.

Prepared like this, lentils can be stored in the air-tight container for about 15 days.

Nutritional values per 100g:

Carbohydrates 19g

Sugar 7.5g

Protein 17 g

Total fat 4.3g

Sodium 188mg

Potassium 72 mg

Calcium 27mg

Iron 5.9mg

Vitamins (vitamin A; B-6; B-12; C; D; D2; D3; K; Riboflavin; Niacin; Thiamin; K)

Calories 123

22. Chia seeds with curry & fresh lime

Ingredients:

3 tsp of vegetable oil

2 tbsp of ginger, freshly grated

2 cloves of garlic, minced

3 carrots, chopped

1 large potato, chopped

1 small onion, chopped

1 cup of dry chia seeds

4 cups of chicken broth

1 tsp of curry powder

¾ tsp of salt

¼ tsp of pepper

lime wedges for serving

Preparation:

Heat oil in large saucepan over medium heat. Add the ginger, garlic, chopped carrots, potatoes, and onions. Saute' until vegetables become soft. Add the chia seeds, broth, and seasonings, stirring well while turning up the heat to medium high until mixture comes to a boil. Cover, turn heat back down to medium-low and simmer for 15 to 20 minutes, stirring occasionally, until seeds are tender and most of the liquid is absorbed. Serve with fresh lime wedges.

Nutritional values per 100g:

Carbohydrates 27g

Sugar 11g

Protein 26.7 g

Total fat 8g

Sodium 598 mg

Potassium 92.1mg

Calcium 41mg

Iron 11mg

Vitamins (vitamin A; B-6; B-12; C; D; D2; D3; K; Riboflavin; Niacin; Thiamin; K)

Calories 182

23. Fresh legumes – mexican way

Ingredients:

1 ½ cups of fresh legumes, chopped

1 ½ tbs of red chili powder or one tbs of Cayenne pepper

1 ½ tbs of onion flakes or 1 tbs of onion powder

¾ tsp of oregano

¾ tsp of garlic powder

¾ tsp of ground cumin

¾ tsp of salt

3 cups of water to start (add more throughout the cooking process)

Preparation:

It is best to soak the legumes the night before. Wash them in a colander and then put them in a saucepan and cover them with plenty of water and let soak for 24 hours. Then drain the legumes. In a large skillet, spread the legumes out and add three cups of water. Add the recipe spices and cook over a medium heat until legumes are soft enough that they can be mashed. You will need to add more water during the cooking process as your legumes will continue to absorb it. Add water a half-cup at a time, just enough to keep the mixture moist with some visible liquid. The entire cooking process will take about 45 minutes. Legumes will be soft to chew. Mash after cooking if preferred.

Nutritional values per 100g:

Carbohydrates 17.1g

Sugar 3.5g

Protein 20.5 g

Total fat 5g

Sodium 568mg

Potassium 81.2mg

Calcium 30mg

Iron 5.1mg

Vitamins (vitamin A; B-6; B-12; C; D; D2; D3; K; Riboflavin; Niacin; Thiamin; K)

Calories 177

24. Lemon shrimps

Ingredients:

1 pound of large shrimps, peeled

2 tbsp of lemon juice

2 fresh lemons, cut into thin slices

5 tbsp of olive oil

½ tsp of sea salt

½ tsp of red pepper, ground

½ tsp of black pepper, ground

1 tbsp of garlic, minced

10 bey leaves

Preparation:

Wash and drain your shrimps. In a large bowl combine lemon juice, 3 tbsp of olive oil, sea salt, black and red pepper, bey leaves and garlic to make a marinade. Soak the shrimps in it. Cover the bowl and leave in the refrigerator for about 10 minutes.

Heat up 2 tbsp of olive oil over a high temperature in a grill saucepan. Fry shrimps for about 15 minutes, stirring constantly. If necessary, add some marinade while frying.

Decorate with lemon slices and serve.

Nutritional values per 100g:

Carbohydrates 11g

Sugar 6.5g

Protein 17.1 g

Total fat 6g

Sodium 232.1 mg

Potassium 53.1mg

Calcium 32mg

Iron 4mg

Vitamins (vitamin A; B-6; B-12; C; D; D2; D3; K; Riboflavin; Niacin; Thiamin; K)

Calories 124

25. Nacho casserole

Ingredients:

1 pound of ground beef

1 small onion, peeled and chopped

1 cup of spicy red beans

½ cup of canned corn, cooked

½ cup of sugar-free tomato sauce

2 tbsp of taco seasoning mix

1 cup of cottage cheese

1 cup of chopped green onions

Preparation:

Cook ground beef over a medium-high temperature, stirring occasionally. This process should take about 30 minutes. Remove from heat and drain well. Cut into bite size pieces and combine with red beans, corn, tomato sauce and seasoning mix. Stir well and simmer over medium heat for about 10 minutes.

Preheat oven to 350 degrees. Pour half of this mixture into baking casserole pan. Top with cottage cheese and green onions and add the remaining beef mixture. Bake for about 25 minutes.

Nutritional values per 100g:

Carbohydrates 27g

Sugar 6.5g

Protein 29.5 g

Total fat 11g

Sodium 611 mg

Potassium 72mg

Calcium 27mg

Iron 6.7mg

Vitamins (vitamin A; B-6; B-12; C; D; D2; D3; K; Riboflavin; Niacin; Thiamin; K)

Calories 198

26. Striped bass

Ingredients:

4 large striped bass

1 tablespoon olive oil

½ tsp of sea salt

¼ tsp of black pepper

1 cup cottage cheese

Preparation:

Combine oil salt and pepper. Use a kitchen brush to spread this mixture over fish. Grill fish over a medium-high temperature, on each side for about 5 minutes. Serve with cottage cheese.

Nutritional values per 100g:

Carbohydrates 9.8g

Sugar 2.5g

Protein 24 g

Total fat 3g

Sodium 112 mg

Potassium 24mg

Calcium 12mg

Iron 2.3mg

Vitamins (vitamin A; B-6; B-12; C; D; D2; D3; K; Riboflavin; Niacin; Thiamin; K)

Calories 143

27. Chicken mix

Ingredients:

2 large chicken fillets, boneless

1 medium tomato, peeled and chopped

1 carrot, peeled and grated

1 onion, peeled and chopped

3 tbsp of olive oil

3 tbsp of sour cream

¼ tsp of salt

Preparation:

Wash and pat dry the meat. Cut into bite size pieces. Heat up the olive oil in a saucepan over a medium-high temperature. Add meat and fry for about 15 minutes, stirring occasionally.

Meanwhile, peel and cut the vegetables into small pieces. Add to the saucepan and mix well with meat. Fry over a low temperature for another 10 minutes, or until all the liquid evaporates. Remove from the saucepan. Add sour cream and salt. Serve warm.

Nutritional values per 100g:

Carbohydrates 24g

Sugar 11.5g

Protein 29.5 g

Total fat 10g

Sodium 462.1 mg

Potassium 63.1mg

Calcium 11mg

Iron 5.6mg

Vitamins (vitamin A; B-6; B-12; C; D; D2; D3; K; Riboflavin; Niacin; Thiamin; K)

Calories 165

28. Steak salad

Ingredients:

1 thin steak

5 lettuce leaves

1 tsp of chopped radicchio

2-3 arugula leaves

4 tbsp of olive oil

3 lemon slices

1 tomato

¼ cup of ground walnuts

½ cup of cottage cheese

¼ tsp of salt

Preparation:

Wash and pat dry the steak. Heat up the olive oil over a medium temperature and fry the meat for about 10 minutes on each side, or until tender.

Remove from pan and soak the excess oil with kitchen paper.Cut it into cubes and set aside.

Wash and cut the vegetables in a large bowl. Add the meat, ground walnuts and cottage cheese. Season with salt and decorate with lemon slices before serving.

Nutritional values per 100g:

Carbohydrates 29g

Sugar 14.2g

Protein 31 g

Total fat 13g

Sodium 602 mg

Potassium 97mg

Calcium 33mg

Iron 11mg

Vitamins (vitamin A; B-6; B-12; C; D; D2; D3; K; Riboflavin; Niacin; Thiamin; K)

Calories 202

29. Seafood - Mediterranean way

Ingredients:

1 small pack of frozen mixed seafood

1 tbsp of olive oil

1 small onion

1 cup of cherry tomatoes

1 tsp of chopped, dry rosemary

¼ tsp of salt

1 tbsp of freshly squeezed lemon juice

Preparation

Heat up the olive oil in a saucepan. Fry frozen
seafood for about 15 minutes, over a medium
temperature (try the octopus, it takes the most
time to tender). You can add some water if
necessary – about ¼ of cup will be enough. Stir
occasionally. Remove from frying pan and allow it
to cool for about an hour.

Meanwhile chop the vegetables into very small pieces. In a large bowl, combine the vegetables with seafood and season with salt, rosemary and lemon juice.

Serve cold.

Nutritional values per 100g:

Carbohydrates 18.3g

Sugar 5.5g

Protein 20.5 g

Total fat 3.4g

Sodium 390.2 mg

Potassium 53mg

Calcium 22mg

Iron 7mg

Vitamins (vitamin A; B-6; B-12; C; D; D2; D3; K; Riboflavin; Niacin; Thiamin; K)

Calories 114

30. Grilled sea bream

Ingredients:

1 fresh sea bream, scaled and gutted

1 bunch of fresh parsley, finely chopped

¼ cup of freshly squeezed lemon juice

4 tbsp of olive oil

¼ tsp of sea salt

Preparation:

Wash the fish, and using your hands soak the fish in lemon juice and olive oil. Grill it over a medium heat for about 15-20 minutes, until nice golden brown color. Remove from the heat and sprinkle with fresh parsley. Serve immediately.

Nutritional values per 100g:

Carbohydrates 10.g

Sugar 2.5g

Protein 23.5 g

Total fat 11g

Sodium 534.2 mg

Potassium 81.2mg

Calcium 32mg

Iron 7mg

Vitamins (vitamin A; B-6; B-12; C; D; D2; D3; K; Riboflavin; Niacin; Thiamin; K)

Calories 170

Made in United States
North Haven, CT
31 January 2023